MATTER

Award Winning Poetry

MATTER

Matter – Oprelle Publications LLC

1. Winning Poetry
2. Soulful Writing
3. Compassion
4. Awareness
5. Healing

Cover Artist, Shatha Alawwad

ISBN 978-1-7357331-5-9

MATTER

Award Winning Poetry

Dedication

This book is dedicated to all the hearts brave enough to share their souls on paper. You are heard and your words live in our hearts.

Much love goes out to each one of you.

Acknowledgements

First and foremost, I would like to thank every person who contributed a poem to the Matter Poetry Contest. Your words touched us very deeply. I would also like to thank team members Frank Vieira, Maren Krizner, Gabby Kolencik, Amanda Beauchat, Jenna Croftcheck, and Allie Lint for all of your hard work, support, and inspiration. Thank you to Shatha Alawwad for the beautiful and intriguing cover art.

Thank you also to our incredible panel of judges, who worked tirelessly and with the most compassionate hearts. Finally, thank you to my family for helping and supporting Oprelle Publishing's mission. Scotty, Nate, Jenna and Ty - everything is possible with your love.

From the bottom of my heart, thank you all for believing that words matter.

Dr. Karen Croftcheck

Table of Contents

Introduction   ix

Compassion

Awareness

Emotion

Humanity

Acceptance

Introduction

Introduction

"the things we feel, the things we notice, the things we write about; it's all evidence of the human paradox. It's proof of what we are. "

-Maren Krizner

"The world of professional writing is big and scary. It's full of people who always seem better than you, looming deadlines, and, worst of all, cover letters. It's a weird industrialization of the most basic of human activities-- creation. The ins and outs of the writing world are, at times, necessary evils. Oftentimes, though, not knowing where to start can hold back even the most passionate writers.

When Karen first approached me about Oprelle, the idea was to create a space for up and coming writers to share their work. I was, of course, absolutely elated. Throughout this past year and the compilation of this book, the importance of expression has become increasingly evident. We received poems from writers of all different levels of experience and walks of life. The ones we have put together for you here were the best among many great pieces of writing.

As you read this book, there is something important I want you to understand: you are holding pieces of these people's souls in your hands. See, I believe that it is impossible to write anything, most of all poetry, without laying oneself bare in some way or another. And the things we feel, the things we notice, the things we write about; it's all evidence of the human paradox. It's proof of what we are.

The world of professional writing is big and scary. Anyone whose undergone the mortifying ordeal of writing a cover letter knows that. But they also know that it is well worth the turmoil. I hope that Oprelle can allow new writers to share their work in a safe, accessible environment. If at least one person who has never shared their work before submitted to this contest, I would consider this endeavor a success. Because we are fortunate enough to be alive and able to share these pieces of ourselves, no matter how big or small.

And that matters.

Sincerely,

Maren Krizner

Submissions Editor/Creative Consultant,

Oprelle Publications LLC"

"There is no art I hold closer to my heart

than poetry."

-   Gabby Kolencik

"There is no art I hold closer to my heart than poetry. Truly, it has been a pleasure to read these writers as they grow in their craft. Thank you to each and every poet for your contribution to this collection, for your vulnerability, and for your continuing love of language. I look forward to reading more from each of you. To our readers, I thank you for believing in us, and for supporting up-and-coming writing; I hope you enjoy and cherish these pages as much as I have."

Gabby Kolencik, Assistant Editor

Oprelle Publications. LLC

"Every single entry we received was heartfelt, and we were sincerely humbled by the raw authenticity."

- Dr. Karen Croftcheck

Wow. Where do I start to say thank you for sharing your souls? When the idea of "Matter" was born, it arose out of a feeling of goosebumps that I had after reading some student poems. Some lucky people have the unique capability of conveying deep emotion in words. How powerful is that?

It is almost as if a door is opened, and we can see inside of a person's actual being. It also occurred to me that the process of transferring feelings into words is cathartic. Hence, our slogan "Write Your Soul" exists. Not only do you help yourself through poetry, but you help others. All poets are part of a unique community of kindred spirits, and I hope your love for poetry continues to grow.

For all of you who shared yourselves and your talents, I want to say a sincere and deep thank you. Every single entry we received was heartfelt, and we were sincerely humbled by the raw authenticity.

Gold finalists are identified, though each has won a either a gold, silver or bronze award from Oprelle Publications. Hence, <u>every poem in "Matter" is from an award- winning poet.</u>

Get ready to feel a range of emotions in the wonderful ride that is "Matter." Enjoy.

All the Best,

Dr. Karen Croftcheck

President, Oprelle Publications

Compassion

Dreams for Hire

**_Dreams for Hire_ is the Second Place Winning Poem.

after Ilya Kaminsky & Jericho Brown

The lives I've chosen to live

Are enough to fill a room with

Newborn birds & ghosts.

Maybe nothing here is lovely.
Or maybe a child is most interesting
When he marvels at the swallow's
Cry for home. Tonight, marks the
First day of spring in glitter.
& I think of the days when the
Accidental blood in my thighs meant
I am still searching for poems that come
Like gentle allies at midnight— a sort of
Ritual that will bring my mother & I closer.
I keep telling myself to walk as if my hand
Can comfort a human sculpture. The people

Of my country believe unhearing is our

Only barrier. I ruffle the pillows & I

Wonder if dancing at our bruises

Is a question of values. All things

Are migratory because we understand

Shadows. We recognize joy & gratitude in

Various stages of intimate. The skies of this

Poem are teeming with human rights & ideology—

I wear my country like a dress. In certain parts

Of the world, my body is an altar in disorder.

An island that smells of iodine & polyps.

Postmodernism is a disguise. Please don't

Take me for tragic. The slatted light betrays

The most animal in us— I am a garland of bells

In this space of Brexit & borderlines. Like when a

Dead child is covered in petals & motherland

Undresses me & recounts: two million

Undocumented children.

-Ojo Taiye

Inspiration

For some time now, I have been interested in using poetry as a form of activism. Earlier this year, I was fascinated or perhaps stricken when I came across this editorial piece.

https://www.theguardian.com/world/2020/feb/09/moria-refugee-camp-doctors-story-lesbos-greece with regards to thousands of vulnerable people living in makeshift tents in Lesbos. I couldn't help but recast their palpable suffering, insidious hopelessness, & the feeling of abandonment. Reading their stories often felt unbearable, yet as much as I wanted to turn away, the desire to give a voice to this silenced people certainly hooked me. Finally, I recently wrote a poem which includes the following one liner; *for the sake of care I write poems until my eyes crater for periods.*

Ojo Taiye

Biography

Ojo Taiye is a young Nigerian poet who uses poetry as a handy tool to hide his frustration with the society. He also makes uses of collage & sampling techniques.

Spinning

My mother started spinning in the orphanage

Her cries echoed from the ceiling

Zig-zagged down the walls

And settled to the creaky floor.

Too many babies. Too few nuns.

Ancient instinct whispered, "Hush up now!

All that hollerin' will only draw predators."

My grandmother, Abenaki? French-Canadian?

Certainly poor, had done what she could.

Overtaxed mammal mothers

Leave their young in lean years.

It's a numbers game.

Stay and they all starve.

Go and she lives to have more in better times.

Nuns in 1950 scooped up abandoned babies

Laid them in wooden cages

Terrified and wanting and waiting for love.

Doing their best to be like Jesus.

But which way is kinder, really?

My mother grew, unheeded.

Made babies at 19

Stumbled and spun through

Marriages, diapers, dishes, alcohol, abuse.

Now she spins resentments into soft grey yarn

She knits us more hats than we can wear in a lifetime.

When she is very old and cries out from her bed,

I will go.

I will feed her and bathe her and rock her to sleep

And she will know peace before she dies.

- Sally Stanley

Otro

Grand avenues jilted with parked envy, wishes, and desperate dreams

Delivered icy gusts sending litter into swirling confetti around a God

Squeezing in with penniless psychotics, alleyway migrants, discharged Survivors, all

French braided together, freezing around fire flaring from trash can braziers.

Numb to the crush of impatient civilization roaring through the bankrupt night at alleys end,

Breath came in gasps as we jostled for warmth and kindness. Otro, a migrant with a

Keen sense of pedigree and restless disaster queried the God about his place at the fire.

As one among us, this threadbare God cadged our heat, with no mention of Those Promises.

Answering with the cadence of Privilege, a fatal tell of unfathomable opportunities,

Failed snipers, grunts, and machine gunners of Every War gathered at the flames,

Glowered at the arrogance of this God, fire flashing off its face like Goya's torches.

Brutal winds blasted trash, scattering a school of white plastic spoons tinkling down our Alley.

Otro shrieked his indictment: "Thermopylae, Agincourt, Normandy, Troy,

Gettysburg, Khe Sahn, Leningrad, Waterloo----Where have you hidden? At Hiroshima, as

Shiva, Oppenheimer's 'Blinding Light.'? Wounded Knee and Auschwitz never saw you! "

The God looked stunned by the migrant's Grasp.

.

Otro's torrent spilled out of him: battles, death, ineffable courage carving the mind as

Thunderstorms sculpt sandstone. We stared the God down, knowing Time erodes the

Tragedy of War leaving those serpentine, sexy, sculpted canyons littered with teetering stacks of

History:

WWII in Color,

The Coffee Table Art of War, Vols. I-II

Vietnam in HD,

Hustler.

Pouting, the Sacred now gushed from the imposter, razor-sharp thorns

Dug into the scalp of the Prince of Pain. Transfixed, we stared with glee,

The God fell clumsily, its Crown toppled, bouncing through indifferent pools of Alley water.

A distant siren spiraled up into the obsidian night, announcing a

New Arrival!

-Richard de Forest

Sticks and Stones

Sticks and Stones

sticks and stones may break my bones

but words will never hurt me

but what if there were no sticks or stones

laying around my childhood home

so the only thing left to hurt

were the words thrown at me

they spilled out of my mother's mouth like a poison

a poison that consumed me

burning, stinging

causing tears to fall

and doors to slam

and horrible memories to haunt me forever

no sticks or stones ever broke my bones

but words broke my heart

it was torture to look at the person who is supposed care for

you

and have so many memories of taking care of them

it is hard to remember the stench of alcohol

on your mother's breath

as you told her everything was going to be ok

it was hard to clean the house

and make the meals

it was hard to raise your brother

and it was hard to not see pride on her face when she looked

at you

but the hardest thing of all

was not being able to be angry at her

because she is fragile

she is breakable

and if she breaks

she cries

and you hate it when your mother cries

so you don't get angry over the tears

you don't get angry over the broken promises

MATTER

you don't get angry at the empty bottles

or the hungry stomachs

or the locked doors

or the words

and you definitely

don't get angry at her

sticks and stones will not break my bones

and words will always haunt me

-Maddie Winther

MATTER

Archaic Trees

Standing there lifeless

Beaten by time

Birds are no longer attracted to thee

Roots are no longer its backbone

Wishing the leaves would cover it

But they have fallen and withered away

That fragile tree

The rain has ignored him

Forsaken by the sun

An outcast to the wilderness

Waiting for its help to come

Help, that it once provided shade for

Standing there lifeless

Still waiting for a return

That lonely, abandoned, tired tree

Our elders

-Latoya Martin

Glass Birds

You never wanted to see another bird

cage clipped bar broken

Not one more crestfallen songstress crooning

for space to unbend wasted wings.

You'd watch the wild ones

singing Alouette by the kitchen window

with a heart unmade for plucking feathers

You loved birds made of milk glass

A flock of frozen white

You made me go through

your bone blanched menagerie

and claim my earthbound angels

when we thought you had

so

much

more

time.

-Amanda Shaw

MATTER

My mother growing up on and away from the family farm

remote; control; on and off

stop signs in dead

corn fields. read silent

by a '69 chevy

nova, butternut yellow

speckled rust -

I am me because

of my suffering,

like the cows, formal

abbreviations

for neglect and cowardice

I am me because of my suffering

The way the crow crows and ships

sail despite the wind

MATTER

Static television,

radio station, saw and head jaggar and richards

sing then, hate it now

like hawaiian shirts from

when that man

taunted quarter-florals and an empty

wallet –

i am my suffering

-Christina Wilson

Awareness

Library of Consciousness

To the ether, to the ether, to the ether I go.

Oh, what shall I find amongst Its' levels and flow?

A song? A legend? A story so sweet?

Or a knowledge so terrible that I should weep?

In Its' emptiness All information behold,

The Occultist's coveted lead into gold.

Searching the expanse of the Singularity's trove,

All Unity's experience, and I, Its' betrothed.

Oh, to feel, to touch, to taste, see and smell,

To experience blissful heavens and the deepest hells.

Betwixt and between reality weave,

A never ending thought moving on Creation's dreams.

I Am, that I Am.

How great, yet how small,

MATTER

Traversing dimensional layers I make the primordial Fall.

To Be, is to be in a time and a place,

Gravity the conductor organizing matter and space.

A symphony of possibility made real and innate,

From the echos of wonder, their coherency's mate.

The orgasmic climax...

Exploding light that birthed the stars,

A cacophony of planned chaos expanding wide and afar.

So why did we do it?

Consciousness, and then awareness I'd say,

Curiosity, the motivation fueled by the urge to play.

To expand, to explore, to seek and to find,

To know every story of the Universal Mind.

And so in the ether, in the ether I know,

The macrocosmic spark that I am here below.

-Christina Wilson

MATTER

The sky falls like needles

The sky falls like needles on the hull

Sails bloated by Poseidon's breath

His trident's thrice-pointed head looks to us

Will this torment last all night?

Goods spoiled and bounty lost

Have we toiled and travelled in vain?

Value of trips outweighed by fear

What gold will scale to the life of a man?

Memories of heroes long forgotten

Odysseus never faced such tumults

What name is on our lips now?

Christ

Fields of wheat and valley hills of green

Sons and daughters and lovers

Homes built of stone, felled trees, and callouses

Left behind for prospects of riches

Tears of heaven or sweat of my brow, I cannot tell

Compasses are of no use now

Call the she-captain, Ana!

She makes her stand 'hind the helm

"Master Ana! Me sees our rudder off the aft!"

"Christ! I, Ana, cannot fight sans rudder. Christ!"

"Aye, Ana, what shall we do?"

Pray

-Matthew McNab

MATTER

Carbon

1

There are people in towers at the mercy of storms,

carbon rain debris to diatoms on ocean floors,

they rise to salt flats and move with dust storms,

flying rivers feed the Amazon floor,

Is our future Mars or Venus?

Heaven is the ache of love, Hell is collective withdrawal,

Is the magnetic field made up of the dying souls of Earth?

entwined protecting us,

or do we become lightning paths in ship graveyards,

Is the space between us genesis?

or the space between the mountains in Peru and sky,

a fight for breath on golden ground,

a graveyard of golden babies,

Is space silent naked noise,

sound captured in the jaws of black holes,

disappearing and reappearing somewhere else,

a protozoa primordial belt in iron playgrounds,

From the soil to the leaves I can feel the water rising,

feeding tree's, a sparkling madness,

MATTER

I can hear the ice breaking, I can feel the sea rising
We stare blankly at blue boxes seeking to fill a void,
until sleep hunts us and collects our dreams,
and stores them in jars across dimensions,
exploding timelessly across deserts and seas,
In pools of space plasma, we lay on cars in fields of green,
under shooting star's, we wish for peace,
and bless the imperfect who look on at trees with
homesickness,
a glimmer of lost reality drowned in the sound of machines,
and the taming of beings,
Can you hear the bells ringing in the shape of the wind?
a call for angels and poets,
a call for ancient stories to merge with the new,
voices exploding like magma to free new matter,

2
We stand between a fiery red and golden light of flashing
heat,
cool craters of the moon drag the sea,
and the cycles of blood and birth,

and in the darkness of thin air we choke on nothingness,

In golden dimensions we sit between the sun and moon,

deciphering the cries of babies and the cries of doves.

-Carly Byrne

"Carbon was inspired by the documentary series One Strange Rock.

I am captivated by the interconnections of Earth and Space matter,

and their possible metaphysical questions."

-Carly Byrne

MATTER

it is only a matter of choice –

it is only a matter of choice

an internal conflict to speak or not to speak

that's the question

pretty rhetorical?

to spill words or to count words

to measure words or to raise words

unspeakably and actively

flush out inactivities of the anti-Hamletian age

the lack of words and some empty promises

the claptrap cliché and the whole word-catching

in the proper common ground

we will harvest uncertain seeds of the silence

small talk no talk about something nothing

about a wheather a cloud on the sky in the heart

about a raindrop a tear on human cheeks

about a new book and controversy between the lines

praised be the freedom of speech

there are so many ways not to speak

so stay silent Ophelia stay silent and mention in your prayers

every human quietness

-Wiktoria

MATTER

Amazonia

Silent death wobbles down dream-like on terrified innocence

Verses of the Gods humming in the heads of the senders

As earnest sacred hatred for those not them, feckless

Shredding of all others, scattering their truth for Millennium.

Differences gathered in two's, three's, and whole Tribes

All with scents and traces of their adored seers,

                              Their truths lay by my bed,
hidden in a scrawled palimpsest

Scarcely heard by Sacred givers of ever more perverse
Miracles.

Drums unseen thunder in the bottomless skin of civilization

Horns blatting in cadence as Robed wardens deny glittering
galaxies,

Shuffling in allegiance to macabre dogmas, their Hymns
bringing giant Soaring half-lidded birds, bearing one more
Colossus of trickery.

My eyes, shifting up or down, glimmer and flutter while
searching for something lost never to be Found. Gods roam
in pastures of myth

Stumbling over veracity laying shrouded in ancient dust,

Silken drapery sits throned, blessed with heralding vague
golden lies.

Life's miracle, bringing one out of two while myth chanted
for Millennium, never challenged, has The-One destroy all in
its path?

Robed arbiters dispense swift vengeance to all who dare.

All is finite but never Lost; there is no Paradise to lose.

Threats to Illusion are found, tried, hung; eddied pendants for mobs

Succumbing to fears of realities beyond the reach of bloodied fists and

Clenched minds. Mysteries bound up in the infinite and finite are

Unleashed: Einstein, Dirac, Oppenheimer, Feynman, Sagan, Dawkins.

All were blinding in their hard found elegance silencing the blaring horns

And tympany of never to be seen Gods with their naked fearful

Accuracy: piercing Myths, False prophets as Bastards, no Father ever.

All the Gods dwindle, dimly lit in an eerie grey glow of deceived corpses.

No Who immaculate or miraculous as Faraday, Clark, then Light.

No Thing more sacred: Scriptures of Math, Gravity, Space-Time.

Painted ceiling Glories shocked pale in the presence of bearded Darwin,

A giant Sphinx

Lays hidden,

Cradled in a deep, lush emerald jungle

Mute,

Wet,

It glistens with fecund Genius and the Sweat of gifted Sapiens.

-Richard De Forest

Night Thought

Woken in the night

coyote song of the successful hunt.

The moon had tipped its last light out

empty gourd laid down on the line of pines

Dawn's headlight haze coming up the opposite hill.

The settled world fires up its tilt-a-whirl.

Off with a vroom and clank and hum

the loud claxon of civilization on the move.

At thirty the body is entire

still as a pond, replete containment

the sky whole in its small ocular.

Later, a draining brook

that floods and dwindles unpredictably

that holds on to nothing

but exchanges its music cheerfully enough

for a bit more pocket-change from the shyster

to whom it all returns anyway,

for his wink and a nod.

-Jennifer M. Phillips

Thermopylae

Swift

Cunning Sapiens

Invade, kill and enslave Eons

before the appearance of Time.

The White Lion, Jim Crow, a heartless Trail of Tears extends
the infinite ledger of

Death.

Smoldering

on distant horizons History also bears witness to ancient and
nascent revolutions,

Throngs awakening from comas of indifference rise from
centuries of deadly apathy;

Eyes riveted on Democracy fluttering in gales of hate held
together with Scotch tape, and

Blood.

The Long Blue Line

Blurring into grainy images of Kristal Nacht stiffens under
glinting towers of glass,

Clout bristling from their smug, leather belts. Sweat soaked
the swarm engulfs the

Architecture of Power boldly kissing the cold stone with
graffiti, the lipstick of

Rebellion:

.

Clouds

of Cotton-white teargas swirl around a shimmering fata
morgana of Justice, eerily

Floating above. Hidden in a cruel palimpsest, visions of
African chattel beaten, raped and hung,

Scorch all eyes and hearts; centuries of sweet Honeysuckle
wafting through the stench of

Plantations.

'The Battle of Algiers'

Rages in my head; its snaring drums the adrenalin of revolutions.

Arms raised into the wind; I crush forward, screaming for those who could not.

Skies darken, suddenly through the blistering clouds of gas, I spot Thermopylae wedged in by

A cerulean blue Aegean,

Waiting.

-Richard De Forest

Rose Glasses

The Sun is red

the moon is purple And trees

are not really green,

the man who walks his dog daily

doesn't really have a dog at all.

See my perception of big can very well be what you

consider quite small.

The sky is not what it seems to be,

clouds are not white they're neon pink

And the girl who speaks to you each day, is no girl at

all, she's actually a he

just soft spoken and not that tall

The things we view with our eyes are not always true,

the eyes tend to play tricks like the mind and heart do.

Stores are not where you purchase food,

those things on your feet aren't even shoes

heartache is not a real, death is alright

And blindness is gifted, perfected sight.

Whereas the young man who came back from war

without his legs,

still dances with his kids every night.

The things that we view with our eyes are not always

true, visions play tricks

like the mind and the heart do.

Divorce is not the end

it is just the beginning

big girls, are the new skinny

A truth is a lie, younger is the new old

& these days HIV is really a bad cold,

The decision

honestly up to you, not me.

Don't ever let anyone convince you that things are

always as they appear to be,

Understanding it's truly your choice to recognize a

rainbow,

in the middle of the street.

Chakuan Jackson

Emotion

Ocean Tears

there is salt

stinging at a million invisible cuts. the hair on my arms

stands at attention.

i shudder. i do not know why i am here.

i don't know how to ground myself in wet sand.

an impossible feat, really. sea foam licks at my toes.

everything changes too fast. i don't remember why i came

here,

but i remember being here with her. her and her laugh and

her seashells and her complaints about her eyeliner and—oh.

there is a gaping hole in my heart. i remember.

somewhere, a light flickers.

when did it get there?

a seagull caws, plaintive.

maybe i am just looking into her mirror, after all.

the sea croons a nameless eulogy and i cannot distinguish

salt-spray from my tears anymore.

-Shriya Sankaran

Inspiration

"Ocean Tears" was a poem I wrote in the process of exploring loss and grief - it's a reflection on the temporal and the fleeting. I find poetry to be a form of catharsis, and a way to safely express emotion that is difficult to confront otherwise."

-Shriya Sankaran

MATTER

 Pastel Landscapes

Pastel landscapes of a pacific skyline drift across the canvas
of my memories

Damp rooms of musky oak linger like smoke

There's nothing wrong with the clock on the wall but I hate it.

(Tick-tock, tick-tock)

Oh to sink my teeth into the leather of your bones

Caress your lips, once more with mine

I'd carry you over the threshold and back,

A thousand times and more

Than to lose the serenity of our time.

Open doored summers with apple blossom perfume, warm
sunspots that dance over blades of grass under a curtain of
leaves

Every sound a chorus,

Every moment a dream

Let me lay swooning while my imagination drifts like
passing clouds.

(Tick-tock, tick-tock)

I am stretched to the limits of my human fabric

Like a flag in hurricane winds

The streets still the same but there's something amiss

Death has called on an errand of bliss

All that is left is the door.

How do you go back?

How do you let the sounds of laughter of comfort?

When does air stop hurting my breath?

(Tick-tock, tick-tock)

Now the Northern lights reflect on winter ice

My eyes reflect your beauty;

Breathtaking

Your sultry smile makes me ache; I am diminished as I stand

before you.

Life is short and if tomorrow's a day that can keep its

distance then I'll be content.

-Raymond Byiers

Cycle of a Breath

Cycle of A Breath

(Part I)   And   (Part II)

i am afraid-	grant me water
my stem will never lift itself up	to quench my thirst,
to You, my	time to solidify
petals will fall	in Your soil,
one by one,	space to unfold
then in droves,	under Your sun,
until nothing remains but	(and) the will power
a devastated bud. i am afraid	to endure—
the thorns thatadorn my outsides will	grant me
color my	(the) sustenance to grow
insides. i long to reach	into a vast, luscious garden
upwards, into You(r)	that nurtures forgiveness,
warmth	that promotes bravery,
but my roots	know(s) healing,
drag me	and breathe(s)
Down –	Kindness.

-Daira Sommerhoff

Cello and Cellist

I am not young but neither are you
As you peruse, second-hand relics the lot of us.
Your touch is not the first but we both stand still,
Hand to wood to hand, silent and knowing.

Traipsing around the city you learn
A new walk, one that encompasses
My bulk on your back. Your body's
Boundaries shift to include me.

I still wonder at the attic where you keep me.
Am I the madness you won't let out?
But I am surrounded by skylights and you
Are the other inhabitant of this strange place.

The first press of the bow is all wrong.
Your fingers shake, for one, and I – cold,
Unused and so afraid this is a mistake.
We are twin cries straining to get out.

We learn, warmed up in an unending embrace.
The pinch of a string pierces air. A single drawn
Out cord, pitch perfect. My trembling and the hitch
In your breath down my neck announces creation

And hours of labour: we mould each other,
Lost and safe in dust dancing in shafts of light.
Between discordant notes is the language
We've always sought, music within touch.

-Marie McMullin

"Someone I deeply admire plays the cello. I owe this poem to her." - Marie McMullin

"*Together*"

The distance between us

Widens, spans beyond time itself

Fills with fire and air

Roars with lapping inferno tongues

Each word we exchange

Is a different fortune teller

And I stand still, bewitched

Waiting for crystal balls to

Drop on my skin

Permeate my pores with translucent glass

That will leave me plastered

With drunken magic from

The otherworld

It feels like an implosive combustion

Is eminent for me

Since I am caught in this in between

That is filled with cold air, deep space

Crystallized saline and

Kinetic heat that burns like the sun

I am powerless to

MATTER

Your erratic magnetic vortex
It will shatter me eventually

And when it does,
I will never be able to
Find my way back
To wholeness in Valhalla
Where we used to reside together

But promise me,
That when the thousands of pieces of me
Fragment
And become golden threads,
You will collect them from the starlit ether
And weave pieces of me into
The edges of you
So that I can still hold you together
When you feel like falling apart

-Jessamy Joy

THANKS FOR THE PTSD, BIG FAMOUS CHICAGO HOSPITAL

This is where I parked, right here, this spot by the elevator

on 'Bing Crosby' as if it grounded me for the day to come.

This is the song, Georgia, that played then, each morning at 5:30

when I got out of the car, already sickened, nauseated

from the moment I saw the Ferris wheel through sunrise

off Navy Pier on the Outer Drive

at the anticipation

of what they might have done to you overnight—and always did.

This is the elevator that led to the bridge,

the bridge that led to the desk where I validated the parking ticket.

This is the ticket that cost too much. Yes.

MATTER

This is the floor, the second floor, with gift shop and
restaurants,

Vietnamese, Vegan, Greek, Au Bon Pain where I bought

Cape Cod kettle chips each night to stay awake

while driving home, crunching them, banging teeth against
one another.

This, too, is the floor where I walked up, down and around,

ascending and descending the pair of escalators each time
around

so legs would carry and heart would pound

for myself and you,

in bed in delirium on a floor I don't remember

with a tube in your throat to breathe

with doctors like vultures saying long term care long term
care

as if hungry for some foul and spoiled food.

MATTER

Over my dead body, I said and exercised in moments I hoped

they wouldn't notice, but they did, and when I left the room
to walk or pee

they came in to do to you what they couldn't when I was
there.

More propofol. More fentanyl. Keep him quiet. Keep him
quiet.

And this: this is the coffee I bought.

This is the table where I sat

for a few minutes on the many days that passed—

This is not how I sat, though, not how alone I was:

this is me being with you now, alive,

you, a little impatient with my memories

because you don't remember,   you don't know   what
it was like

or know why even seven years later I watch

for the tall lean doctor in his fancy suit

and dream of hitting him,

hurting him, hurting, hurting, hurting him

until he cries out,

What did I do to her?

-Carol Coven Grannick

Inspiration

"This poem evolved the first time I returned - almost 6 years later - to the hospital site where my husband had a nightmarish experience for 7-1/2 weeks. They assumed he would die and I had to do whatever I could, with the help and support of my family and friends, to make sure that didn't happen. I still have some PTSD, but my husband, who was long unconscious, does not. I'm grateful for that."

-Carol Coven Grannick

Burial

Rain weighs down the earth.
Each clear ring of the spade slicing
through mud sends shockwaves
along my arms, rippling across
the years to come and those gone by.

I roll the body into the pit,
hear its wet fall into sludge.
I pile back the earth – easier
than digging. I tap the mound smooth,
three times to call for peace.

Useless pandering. You crawl out,
or I crawl in, obnoxious persistence incarnate.
Amidst harsh breaths, fast and mad,
questing fingers with dirty nails find
a face, trembling in the grave I have made.

Were I to peel the skin from your skull,

MATTER

Would in find the same as in mine?
– Dreams that never breathed, potent
like memories; neural patterns nonetheless,
grief-carvings hardwired in the brain.

                              -Marie McMullin

" I have a rather good memory, which is useful in many
circumstances. Sometimes, though, I wish I were better at
forgetting." - Marie McMullin

My Knees are Weak

I sent you a pet today

She kept me company since you discorporated

I didn't expect to bury her tonight

How can I fill the grave

Throw dirt where she lays...

when I can't even say goodbye

I held her in my hands

I knew at first glance

Ohh something was wrong

Thumb rubs back and forth…

While my mind begs me to let go…..

Oooh how can I put her down

Knowing that this moment

Is the last we'll ever have?

How can I look awayKnowing she won't be there

when I look back

MATTER

Noooo....

Every place I look,

Memories, they flash

But only I'm here to remember that

All of the time spent, nothing can be said...

I only want my choicest friend

Oh the wretched pain, Like abandoning...

Only I don't even have

Comforting knowing that

Your on your separate path

No I know that

Life has rolled on

Leaving you behind

now here I stand

At the end of your path

How am I supposed to

MATTER

Step on from your bitter end

Knowing that you can't

What have I done to deserve to breathe?

And all the willing can

Never bring you back

I can't stand to be alone with me

I know that we will all cease to survive

I know that the soul is the mind

I don't know where, but I know your gone

The world feels lighter now

No guarantee, as to where you've gone

Why

Why

Why

Must you leave

Where could nowhere be

-Laney Rivenbark

Interlude

Burned atop a roof

A sunset in the distance,

Golden and orange and low,

The stench of smoke,

The smell of a breeze,

The flame licks on and on and

On the crown of a forgotten tower,

She untangled with the heights of damnation.

-Isabel Chave

Wasteland

In the midst of the gray and misty swamp

Lay broken china dolls,

Broken language,

A broken marriage-

-that, like a phoenix,

Birthed a renewed friendship-

Dog-eared books and new ones awaiting oily fingers

Abandoned ideas left for brighter ones

A broken heart resulting in the most complete version

Of a once-lost girl.

Whispers of

Sana sana colita de rana

Run with the wind.

Sitting on Campbell's Soup Cans,

Peering in the mirror,

As if it were A Set of Six Self Portraits

Each of them being a vastly different version of myself.

A pandemic spreads as rapidly as the wildfires

Yet I am empty inside;

I am not feeling the emotions I am expected to feel.

MATTER

"Who is underneath the bed?"

He demands as I peer from the steps

On the day our savior was born.

I listen to slow breathing

As whirring machines beep.

"Mi muñeca linda"

The Kaiser curls up next to me

So that he is not lonely,

And so that I am not cold.

So filled with love, brimming with curiosity,

Not unlike the redheaded Anne of Avonlea

But the hour for rest has come.

Good night, moon.

Mr. Mojo Risin watches me as I sleep-

the lizard king himself

who died his glorious death in the city of love-

As I am transported through the universe

To a place as real as the Earth I am on now.

With closed eyes, I explore

These experiences called *dreams*.

But oh, they are so much more.

-Tatiana Cleffi

Under Your Fingers

On a chair
in the middle of the room
you are playing strings
looking beautiful

The room
a simple cathedral
filled with music
from under your fingers
and in the middle of the room
you
looking like you do
immersed in a world
a thousand years old and new

Fresh air coming in
I can see it
touching you
I can see it
stroking your beautiful face
I can see it
dancing around you

MATTER

and you don't know
immersed in your world

My soul
under your fingers
a thousand years old and new

The freshness of the moment
in this simple room
air touching your face
my eyes touching you.

                    -Michaela Achelis

Severance

Asteroides, according to Linnaeus and his ilk.

Common sea star, that
commonly loses
its limbs.
A severed limb
grows back
for *Asteroides*. Not for you.

Seas rise
with the tide
with the moon
with the stars.

Your toes traced stars in hot sands
on Pacific beaches.
I think of Coronado.
Salty surges lapped your two (2) feet,
Toes licked by leaving tides
But that was then, before the bitter bacterium and
the severance of

leg, foot, toes.

Step on a crack.

Break.

Asteroides, how do you do it?

Sea star whose severed points

regenerate,

Who grows limbs anew.

Limbs as good as new,

of sea-fed star-flesh.

Not of silicon.

Prayers sink into the sea

Unanswered, and yet

Still we believe

in regeneration.

In generations and generations

of daughters, of love,

of stars. Of *Asteroides* and its ilk.

Resurge. Rise again, like a sun, like a star.

Surge with silicon strides: your good steps.

Resurge, effulgent one. *Resurge.*   -Leslie Carlin

Inspiration

"I wrote the first draft of my poem, "Severance," to express sadness about the suffering of someone I love. As time passed, and suffering turned to strength, my sadness became admiration and hope. The poem, I hope, reflects that trajectory. Its title, suggested by a poet friend, almost tells the story by itself."

Leslie Carlin.

Understanding

I am From

I Am From

I am from the Paw-Paw Patch and

Tura Lura Lura.

I am from the first lightning bugs in June,

the drone of cicadas, and the smell of

humid San Antonio scorchers.

I am from empty glass milk bottles

in a metal crate left on back porch steps.

I am from roller skates with a key and

Gramps's hand for the steep places.

I am from a musty, creepy garage

with a black gangster car.

I am from a creaky glider on the front porch and

Gramps's lap in the big rocking chair.

I am from pinto beans and cornbread,

and Angel Food cake every birthday.

I am from Vacation Bible School, Jesus loves me and

all the little children, and Popsicle stick shepherds.

And…

MATTER

I am from you're nothing special and

you disgust me.

I am from anxiety, fear, desolation---but

never able to speak it.

I am from two lives: my once-home,

and then my never-felt-like-home,

attempting escape into safety

found only in the Bookmobile on Tuesdays.

-Aisha Claire Robins

Don't Forget Your Thank You Cards

You're fourteen or fifteen and it's Christmas at your grandmother's house.

In the living room that you'll dream about years later you gather with your brothers and cousins for gifts.

No shoes on the nice white chair your father instills in you as his father instilled in him.

Each box has a lovingly written name on it, your grandmother's strict Catholic school cursive.

She must have made a mistake though because the bag with your name on it has an iTunes gift card that you have no way to use.

You've received your gifts out of order and your moment of confusion melts into grateful awe as you open a small box with an iPod Nano inside of it.

There is glowing musical square that you hadn't imagined owning and a few hours spent in your grandparent's guest room where they keep their computer on an old wooden desk.

Your grandmother helps you download your favorite rock n roll albums that you'll later be embarrassed by.

She likes some of the band names and tells you her approval when she does.

The car ride home is split between excited family conversation and a tentative musical experience all of your own.

You are blessed and will remember the love that surrounded you even as you go through the harsher environments of your life.

Soon you'll figure out how to make playlists.

-Levi Donaldson

Blossoming

You are a budding rose,

Blossoming;

An emblem of beauty,

you dance through the Earth's lips,

swaying hither and thither

through the

crumbling

soil.

Induce the swirling wind,

Or the gushing rain,

Thou has been through enough toil.

MATTER

Submerged in water,

She struggles to be free,

but be patient,

blooming flower,

Here comes a wandering bee.

As the rage subsides,

and

her leaves

fall

There, amongst the fields,

Blossoming

The flower still stands tall

-Alissia Nicholas

The Dune

The sun was high in the sky, the land barren
and dry, Sand tangled their hair as they
roamed,
puffs of grass grew, in the southward wind
they blew, While opposite the crystal water
foamed.

The boisterous boys both sunburnt, strolled the beach with
comfort, As fine shells crushed beneath their feet,
The beach was empty, untouched for many a
century, And the secret realm was left to
flourish in the heat.

In the distance they saw it, as if waiting there
dormant, A huge sand dune emerged from the
ground,
Lined by paper bark trees, as if begging on
its knees, For a challenger to be crowned.

It was a nasty race, pushing and shoving after
each pace, The unspoilt sand turned to a bomb
site,

MATTER

Each stride left a dent, as the rivals built their
deadly ascent, both determined to go down with a
fight.

As the summit drew near, their motive was
undoubtedly clear They raced for their pride,
Their honour, their reputation, both were born for this
exhilaration, Matching each other stride for stride.

The Race had been won, but not all were
having fun, The defeated was sombre,
His hot head hung, his facial expressions glum,
As he settled on the sand to ponder.

Then the answer came, as fast as summer rain,
The race wasn't lost yet
Ascending was half the race, down was the
full chase, he'd have to take the bet.

The race was back on, and just as rapidly the boys
were gone, Sand moved with their feet as they
darted,

Sweat glistened in their hair, as air screamed past in
a blare, Both sped towards the finish line
wholehearted.

Then it was done, the loser had won,
The duel had been drawn,
foes were friends, and had made amends,
Their friendship would live on.

Now they think back and remember the
sacred place, where the sand played with
their hair,
Where the unpruned trees, rustled in the breeze,
And know it will forever be safe there.

-Roc Palmos Woodhouse

Shall I call you friend star shine –

Shall I call you friend star shine,

Or moonbeam lover?

Walk with me, hand in hand under the cloudless night,

Let's tell stories of our past lives until the morning light.

Shall I call you falling raindrop,

Or morning dew?

Come with me into the darkness, the shadowless night,

Let's strip naked and swim in the waters of delight.

Shall I call you crimson sweetheart,

Or snowflake morning?

Dance with me around the fires of truth,

the burning mind,

Let's fall together into the vastness of eternities night.

Shall I call you golden sunshine,

Or blue bird sky,

Lie with me on the beach of the eternal mind,

Sands smooth and white,

Let's die to everything imaginary leaving only the souls

eternal light.

-Robert Frederich

In the quiet places...

Blushing tree tops,

shadowless side walks,

railroad trains and rain drops.

All of the answers to yesterday's questions

arrive quietly.

All of the voices of yesterday-

silenced by the coronation of the sunrise.

She awakes into windowless light,

mercies are shining,

the past veiled in white.

She's a dancer in a day dream,

a child with a kite.

In the cool damp quiet,

her companion sleeps.

White mittened paws,

eyes big blue moons,

heart bursting with love.

This is her salvation.

She looks for love in loud places,

but she forgets the gaps,

forgets the small spaces-

the things that simply exist,

and exist simply.

Unconditional love seeps through the smallest cracks

of the sidewalk in the morning.

It rises into the air,

and gathers molecules to itself

like a bouquet of flowers.

    It disperses itself

and gathers itself,

        disperses

and gathers,

and then slips away

to quiet hearts

in the gracious arms

of sleep,

where love and pain are clothed

in dreams

           -Denise Varnedore

Lantern of happiness

If it was possible

to let everything out of my hands

gracefully

like a small paper ship on water

Blow and say

I am not holding you

You belong to the water

to the wind and the ducks

Swing

rock

and discover new worlds

there behind the reeds

If it was possible

to let everything out of my hands

with nobility

like a Chinese lantern of happiness

and say

I am not holding you

Fly with the wind and the Sun

beyond the horizon

MATTER

Maybe you will wake up
the pink hope there

If it was possible
to let everything out of one´s hands
without cracking the wise heart.

=Michaela Achelis

As a Mountain

My memory reaches back millennia.

As a mountain I stood tall and proud.

My soul had the freedom to run in the lush thick foliage that
encased my skin.

Lakes in the valleys below drank from my sweet streams.

Streams that came out of the deep from playful springs that
bubbled up

and gently caressed itself down my side.

Oh, to hear the birds!

Their beautiful tones ringing across my glades.

I stretched north and south, my domain was grand.

To friends and family, I had no greater connection, their arms
reaching mine.

I loved the clouds that combed my peaks.

I would peer over as they split upon my face.

At night I could look up in the heavens, the purest of beauty.

Stars upon stars would smile down on me.

I reveled in the conversations I had with my friend, the wind.

He would roar down my canyons and all who heard were
astounded.

The joy I had as a mountain!

As things go, nothing lasts.

So is my tale and so is my fate.

Now, I am nothing more than the past.

A lonely outcrop, nothing more than a crag.

My soul can no longer run free and is stuck in mere meters.

Over the years, my beautiful streams cut me.

They grew beyond their means and carved me away.

My friend the wind, cut me off from my family. I was left

standing alone.

Year after year I could feel my life shortened.

The only voices I hear comes from the wind.

He threatens me with every breath, year after year he wears

me down.

I see my family in the distance. Their shadows, the only thing

that now connects us.

Oh, what heights they have managed! I cannot take it!

I can't stand tall! I can't be majestic! I have lost all

grandeur!

The clouds mock me with their height.

MATTER

The stars evade me and only a glimpse of the dimmest of
stars keeps me sane.

Why could I not be made of granite, of basalt or even
limestone.

But no, I was doomed to be sandstone, threatened by every
wind and rain.

Now in my days I lay in the desert basin of what was once
my great domain.

I consign myself to my doom. I am only to become a forgone
word.

I am only to be, in the past, as a mountain.

-Nathan Dorathy

To Beat the Clock

It was a race in simplest terms, a race against the clock.

An effort to get from point A to point B, before time ran out.

A treasure hunt through an obstacle course, clock counting down,

When time ran out, it all was over.

She had been told from her earliest memories, that life would be short,

Shorter for her than it would be for others.

If she was to accomplish her goals, fulfill her dreams and reach her destination,

She had better get after it.

Like anyone there were obstacles and roadblocks, detours to where or what she wanted to be.

But time for her would be more precious.

So she moved forward, as quickly as she could manage,

Gathering what treasures she could, reminded

constantly that her clock was winding down,

Faster than the others along the way.

A murmur doctors somberly reported at her birth.

A severe heart defect, one that children did not survive for long.

In the most optimistic of prognoses she might see her seventh birthday,

That was the best one could hope for.

Providence, courage, perseverance, simple twists of fate

Allowed her to exceed those expectations.

But not without the ever nagging presence of her demise chasing after her,

Lurking in the blind spot somewhere just behind her, over her shoulder,

Just below the surface.

So she anxiously raced forward,

Grasping at every passion her strength allowed.

Hurriedly trying to fit an entire lifetime,

Into whatever time was granted.

It's so very rare to know in advance the time of one's
passing.

Life is so tenuous.

One can't be certain of seeing another day, yet we go about
life as if we'll live forever.

Tomorrow promises another chance,

Or so it seems

But imagine if you will,

Living a high-wire balancing act, between life and death,

As she did.

Attempting to fulfill ambitions and dreams, in an uncertain
timeframe.

And what it truly means to race,

To beat the clock.

-Jimmy O'Meara

An American Haibun

Mini-flocks of eight or ten wild parrots often emblazon the trees in my yard. A stopover en route to or from the Home Depot parking lot. As though picking up supplies for ongoing nest repair.

Green red and yellow
packages slur the airwaves
Jingle of chatter

Today bells ring the sky from blocks away. The entire flock arrives as I close the front door behind me for my walk. The surreal surprise of sixty-some parrots. Bodies built for South America that have branched the skies of Northern California for thirty years. Their evolution from a few slave-traded rebels and rejects. And their sheer spirit for survival stops me mid-step.

Ornaments on palm
filbert cherry blackberry
Breeze of wings folding

I refuse to relinquish either the exercise or the parrots. So I walk fast circles around the driveway. Tree-to-tree talk, as affable as small town gossip over clotheslines. Drowning

echoes of the morning's Mercury crime-corruption-jobless-

foreclosure-war News . . . and the crinkle of worry by fingers

on

fabric over a breast lump.

Beaks fill with nectar

from eucalyptus blossoms

Bright pink petals fall

Dizzy now, I switch to a house-wide back and forth stride.

Envision that every Silicon Valley soul in torment could line

up right here. Like the way back-to-belly cars parade slowly

around this cul-de-sac

to see Christmas lights.

Sprinkler shower play

Parrots groom one another

The sun sends glitter

Every feather a rainbow. Every squawk an upbeat, a

hallelujah. An invitation to plan the next thirty years. Even

the native crows acquiesce their territory to this gift. But it is

I who am repaired.

-Ellaraine Locke

Courage

Apathy (the heaviness of the hand)

I never thought that a person's hand could weigh so much.

But then, I've never seen a hand raising a revolver, or ready to slap

a face in betrayal. I've never seen one scattering soil over the grave

of a three-year-old, or caressing someone unloved, I haven't seen

one writing a last latter, or holding another, departing hand. So, they say,

I don't have the right to gather such weight in my ulnar and radial bones,

they say, I don't have the right to consider my carpal bones unmovable.

I know I must move these hands for the sake of those stuck in their beds,

breaking out in pigmental blemishes, having lost everything,

or for those who lost their limbs to shrapnel, whose hands now belong

to the eternal ecosystem. Splayed over the edge of the bed,

on a frayed

bedspread, despite my self-scoldings, arguments, ultimatums,

I can't even caress my child's head – my hand hangs heavy,

for, it seems,

as soon as I touch it, that same soil will fall on him as well. I

struggle

with myriad black forms, blood that won't flow into ten little

fingers,

but if I am called, if I need once more to hold on for the road,

I promise you

my hand, world, to find a brief respite from this unearthly

weight.

-Lina Buividaviciute

Translated by Rimas Uzgiris

Inspiration

"Apathy (the heaviness of the hand)" is from the special
cycle called "Syndroms." - Lina Buividaviciute

MATTER

enlighten me to the world

enlighten me to the world

my fears wish to conceal

search out the identity

I left discarded in the field

where I lost the battle of wills

unlay it from its rest

and help me sew the frayed ends

to my tattered soul

breath warm air

on my frigid lips

and thaw the coldness

I wrapped around my heart

be my shelter

while I endure the storm I tried to numb

allow my tears to create a downpour

MATTER

that results in the grace of acceptance

and show me the kindness

I have not learned to give to myself

-erin michelle

Death Song

When the protagonists love dies she holds him in her arms
and sings
It's a law of the musical universe
This unbreakable line of steel etched over paper and ink
The rest can bend and burn and break
But when every second chance you sold your soul for
sublimates into icy smoke
The death song will be there
For minutes, or hours, or years
Waiting to be sung like the last bullet in a chamber bearing a
name
You could never bring yourself to utter because
Calling them anything but "Love" felt like lying

There's one waiting for all of us
Lines of music written like a scythe cutting waterfalls of tears
Into a curtain you could stand under and stay dry
Carving initials into the rock wall of history so deep
That a thousand lines of spray painted mocking laughter
can't erase them

Leather pants and rubber smiles pull back my hair hard
enough
That I can almost believe these are gasps of pleasure not pain
I just have to close my eyes and lean in a little more
See he never dies till she's done singing
They never walk out the door that last time
Until there's nothing left you need to tell them
So I will ALWAYS have more I need to tell you

I need to tell you how the knife edge of your smile cuts ink
from my veins
Splatters broken promises on to my page
Better than any needle ever could
How the grains of sand caught in your laugh lines
From the night we made love with the ocean together
Were the only thing I ever found more beautiful than
whiskey
How there are a million burning stars caught behind your
eyes
And I would-have-will set my soul alight

MATTER

For the barest breath of a chance to melt the locks you built

to keep them chained

How I will never let this song be over because you can't

leave me again

You can't

You c-

-

-

-

-Jordan Abronson

Smoke Signals

<u>***Smoke Signals* is our First Place Winning Poem</u>

I

of course you carried the fire

grandmother, remember, you could read smoke.

in another life you danced wild against the onyx
sky that made a home in your eyes.

you magic woman,

transcriber of stories passed through the eternal

naval, I placed my hands in the center

and a thousand fingertips reached back

to meet me in the womb I've yet

to be pulled from.

II

grandmother who had rivers for veins,

can you lead me to the gulf?

I am waiting for the world to open

like you waited for men in white coats

to give you air to breathe

in a world where there was none left.

the disease appeared in you
like a warning, you said, but in a language
no one understood
the invasion that only you felt
until I was birthed in your image—
destined to tend the coals.

III
this is what it means to be woman.
a flint blade clenched between teeth
and a womb full of stones, heavy as
eternity. fear, my holy birthright,
unmovable horizon I am always
approaching— autumn, season
of decay. teach me how to begin
again. the earth took this body back
but now I can only breathe mud.
I give myself to the flames now, a desperate
attempt at purification—¬ if I must—
God, I would rather burn than rot.

MATTER

IIII

speak to me through the folds of time.

tell me again of red cedar and sage

and divinity unlearned. an alchemy woman

taught me the importance of surrendering

to trauma's perpetual current and I floated

back to you. there are stories stuck

in the back of my throat, larvae waiting

for metamorphosis. make moths of them.

take me back to the root and I will weep

blossoms, for you, grandmother.

and for all of us after.

-Kate Furlong

During Native American Sweat Lodge ceremonies,
participants enter a small enclosure and sit around a sacred
fire. The ceremony is broken up into four sections or
"doors", each growing in intensity, to honor the four
directions. After the fourth section, participants emerge from
the dark lodge and into light, representing liberation and
leaving behind all that is impure.

Katlyn (Kate) Furlong, Winning Poet

Katlyn (Kate) Furlong is a graduate of California University of Pennsylvania where she received her BA in English with a concentration in Creative Writing. Kate continues her education at the University of Metaphysics where she is studying spiritual healing. She has been published in Red Cedar Review and Litro Magazine. Kate works as a teacher but lives as a student.

"Smoke Signals" is from her collection based on healing intergenerational trauma.

MATTER

Parted

There are no jagged edges snagging at

The little pieces of me

As they flake off as useless reminders

Of what I forgot.

Everything is smooth, instead,

Soft and rounded.

It would be better, perhaps,

If it would show.

Maybe if I ran my hand through

The memories of blackened dust

Along my cranium,

It would catch on sharp thorns

And tear the flesh right from me

And I would bleed the proof of my pain

Onto the floor

So that no one could deny its

Existence.

But I am left with pliant fixtures

And walls thin as silk.

I am capsuled by a thousand intents

With the power to choose

And I can only decide to kill them.

I am ravished. I am barren.

I am burned up from within

And it was the match that I stroke

That vanquished me.

I set the fire but could not hold the flame.   I am gone
without ever having left.

-Madison Slusher

Viola

That evening
the world was tired
of its own charm
The town was falling asleep
into a restless sleep
and every moment
it started from a dream
Who knows which nightmare it was?

That evening
the world was tired
of her beauty
when she was walking alone
down the docks
Yes, everything must happen one day
and we can blame the law of diversity
Just pull the hair and press the fingers
against the throat

That evening

for the last time
the old eyes of the harbor
sucked in the graceful moment
that youth
life

because everything in the world
keeps changing
Just screw the arms behind the back
and push to the ground

That evening
the world was tired
and the town that was sleeping

-Michaela Achelis

ON

There's a little town not too far from the one I live in

Where the sky lights up old

with indigo, amber, and gold

The song that the poor child carries

Transcends painted faces

With delight of the unknown

The dream and regret left behind troubles

Who plagued the oak valley near New Orleans

When rubble nearly satiates the anguish

Destruction offers the sentiment of serenity

To sharpen our silver tongues and dirty paws

So that they might sever

the tether that binds us so

In relenting, to fight against the current

Waves of wise might push us onward

Towards home

My vindication I might offer, unrequited

For a hero must relinquish time in his wake

Sail broadly into depth of an insatiable horizon

Or simply retire an anchor to his weight

-Elia Harper

Humanity

only to have it drown in its own wax

"To err is to human," the fortune cookie states. And self-

forgiveness is fine,

but what if I'm the one who is killing

myself? My life is in cobwebs,

and a shadow in the shape of my mother is wielding a broom

in the attic. Meanwhile

her footsteps echo in the hallway and here is the crucial part

of this story:

I am both the kid

cowering under the covers

and the monster

underneath the bed.

(Somewhere,

a girl lights a candle.)

-Michael Li

Inspiration

"I've always wanted an attic when I was younger. The idea of a place like that, at the top of the house, right above the ones you love but separated from them in some inexplicable way, attracted me very much. A shelter and a cage all in one. What is writing if not turning the metaphorical into the literal? Only in your mind, yes, but it is only there can you confront reality. After all, what is the mind if not the attic of our hearts?"

- Michael Li

Ashes

He's been to this Starbucks before

Someone at a nearby table says

he rotates to avoid arrest

A mountain man or maybe Santa Claus look

Except skinny as a stage-four Jesus

Guitar on top of his grocery cart

over piles of clothes and a bag of cat food

Cat food for Christ's sake, when there's no cat

Twenty-six degrees last night and damp

Yesterday it was a moth beating against

the outside glass

A feverish fight for survival

that I instantly knew I'd assist

But my mental clock ticks slower now

In considerations about connecting

to a man without roots

One who could become a daily complication

Minutes pass that prefer moths

before the man leaves his cart

MATTER

and heads for the alley

An image of dumpster food replaces denial

of my Montana heritage that decrees humane as religion

Mountain Man returns from the direction

of the Mobile station with a pack of Camels

Rips off the plastic and lights one up

Burning with it the sandwich I was about to buy him

and the conscience that forbade my vanilla bean scone

When I walk to the car

his head and back bend over guitar scratches

that no one would ever pay to hear

At home I sweep up the ashes

Moths that chose flames

Salem cigarettes and Valium prescriptions

smoldering in my past

The day has disappeared in smoke

-Ellaraine Locke

Nothing Else

In the horror of breathtaking happiness

a brief look at the order of things

and then a shrunken heart

drown in the notion of the possibility

that the structure of the world

and the transparency of the air

could perish.

Just a floating something

Just a body squeezing its way

through a thick shapelessness.

Nothing else.

                              -Michaela Achelis

 *Oil Painting*

The little girl's holding a butterfly net.
There's a gloved hand on her shoulder.
Stalin in the flowering grasses.

-Roger Craik

"I saw a propaganda painting of Stalin with children in a book I took out of the local library. The poem, if it is one, came to me after I'd been staring at it."

- Dr. Roger Craik

MATTER

On Another Plane of Reality

A beat of a moment stares back at me.

Somewhere in history we've locked eyes,

A moment of a beat gone by

And now we walk amongst each other with echoes for souls,

Unsure children aching at the infancy of recollection long
past

Our fires are root within each other, and

When my eyes might flutter shut, will you be there when I
wake up?

A beat of a moment goes by;

Lightning strikes.

A flame kindles in its place

Somewhere-somewhen,

In another life,

I have waited ages for you.

Isabel Chavez

Chameleon George

Chameleon George,

Suavely moving in and out amongst the people, working the crowd.

Accepted and admired as he spouts his uninspired intelligence.

Blah, blah, blah, the textbook words from his tongue,

Laughing, gaily the people drink,

Drinking in the celebrity of his distinguished normalcy.

The social norm, a true triumph of the age.

An age of lemmings.

Following, ever following the loudest, or prettiest one.

An age of chameleons.

Hiding, ever hiding the light within, hiding in plain sight, totally unseen.

The age of evolved animals, but still the hunter and the hunted.

Years pass, become decades.

George alone, 'kills', sleeps, and eats his way to the top of the social order.

But alas, at the top there is no order,

Only internal chaos as he discovers the top is barren,

The achievement fruitless, the pursuit of his 'happiness' foiled.

The parties no longer need him, there is someone louder now.

Aging was his obsolescence, no longer as captivating in wrinkles and chin rolls.

George now sees he is a vagabond from his own soul,

Spiralling down the gullet of social oblivion.

Clawing with worn claws at the maw that has consumed him,

Struggling to break free from behind the monster's teeth, whom he sought and served,

George cries out with all his whit and wow, to gain some outside aide...

But the socialites social on...

Laughing, drinking in the next soul to drain dry.

George has no substance to call on, no colours of his own to parade,

For he merely copied the colours and swagger of others,

And so he left no memorable mark, nor had a reason he be spared.

George sighs. He has no meaning. He resigns.

He is not a glass half full or half empty kind of guy...

He's just empty.

All because George chose the life of a chameleon.

-Christina Wilson

Logic of the Non Sequitur

Revenge is a dish, like albatross,
best offered and served with tea.
Hate's the emotion, like applesauce,
sweeter than it has right to be.

Sadness is like a marriage,
a way of never saying goodbye.
Tears anoint your face with courage,
but argue it's time to cry.

Anxiety, a frosted blight,
serves none but those it frees.
Fear creeps in on godless nights,
when dreams provide no ease.

Living makes no sense to the dead,
who have no tears to dry.
Dying, like a dog seeking its' bed,
circles before it lies.

-G. Greene

MATTER

Frames

I try to see things fresh and new

to discover hidden meanings

and learn their inner truths

I try so very hard

but all I see is their thingness

surface symbols become surrogates

artifacts detached from archetypes

a continuity of conformities

a way of things so commonplace

they are furniture

decorating the houses of my life

the cat knows they are just things

but believes they all belong to him

barreling from room to room

confirming their persistence

in the palace of his possessions

until he pauses

to sharpen his claws on them

carving his marks in the veneers of time

until he stands

to tear at the blinds

to see what things of his

lay beyond the window

until I pick him up

to keep him from destroying them

and pet him long enough to calm him

or at least distract him

until I can set him down again

to go back to my work

the blinds once more preserved

-Kevin Sandefur

MATTER

What We Wear

A pair of knee-high socks,

A damp towel,

A poker face in a game of cards.

A job title,

awarded by a man wearing an overpriced blazer,

a tie tied too tight.

A pair of grass-stained, sweaty cleats.

Our hearts on our sleeves,

blue ink from a bleeding pen,

staining the tips of fingers.

A smile.

A hand knit sweater from grandparents on Christmas,

with stitched on tabby cats, and "peace, love, joy",

a promise to wear it for every holiday.

backward, a red soxs ball cap,

glittery blush pink nail polish.

A uniform,

a disguise,

a lie.

Overused sentences

and beaded friendship bracelets,

we wear out people like tire treads,

wear out ourselves

with apologies and regret.

We wear out tight dresses on city nights,

pocket watches,

crumbs on our chin.

Seatbelts

blankets in the backseat of the truck,

killer heels.

-Hannah Murphy

Puppets of God

Heads suspended in the air

Hung by strings connected to a single wooden board

They slowly sway to and fro

Their eyes hollow pools of liquid, blind

Frozen in a single frame of mind

As deformed mouths spit empty arguments

Their ideations hold no sense

Massive contradictions hang below their lips

Each side is aware of this

They hear

But never listen

And I must sit between them

Chained by a single rule to my seat

They defy everything I believe and value

And in turn I rage

MATTER

To them I am lost and delusional

Perhaps even possessed by evil

But I am the only sane one

My pastor preaches that to be free

We must be confined within a fence

Inside the fence we can do whatever we please

No need to be afraid,

Though we will fear anyway

Of course we are always free to leave

But if we do, we face death

We have free will

But no choice

Can you believe that this fence represents truth?

Aren't we only herded into fences for denying the truth?

My wrath is ignited when these people prop themselves

On pedestals

When I see their true nature

MATTER

I see the judgement

And they think I don't

To be God is to need validation

To have narcissistic injury holding the infinite mass of the universe

To chase after one reason

To be proud of creating something detestable

The human race is a mistake

He knows that

And I know that

And we seem to be the only two

So I am left wondering what is real,

And what is mere simulation

Generated by organized religion

Nonetheless,

I will not pretend to agree

I will not succumb to the teachings of the cult

MATTER

I will not sing to a cloud of gas

So I cut the strings

Smash the board

And burn them

Heads and all

-Kaitlan Zook

On My First Day of Teaching, I Rethink My New Career

It didn't happen the way the experts had conceived.

They'd pictured a vertical blast, steam and ash

erupting in a plume, a messy but minimal

reordering of the slopes—not this lateral blast,

boulders flung like skipping stones,

mountain melting like candle wax,

billows that rose fourteen miles,

scientists scrambling to interpret clouds,

ash that rained and choked, turning morning to night,

sludge of soot, snow melt, felled trees rolling like fate,

total destruction and re-creation of all they'd studied

and believed they'd understood.   - Jane Sasser

MATTER

With so many books

With so many books I choose almost broken ones

or maybe they don't start that way.

Sides a little lifted

stitches a little torn

Black and White comprehension come stained with coconut

oil but I still pick her before the pretty ones.

In embedded in her I feel comfortable.

Knowing her purpose just the same

holding my treasures, increasing visions, growing from old

hurts.

Pretty books often bring staggering pens.

-tabatha

Bury me in solid concrete

Bury me in solid concrete-
Submerge me in the Mariana.

Carry me among the stars.
I submit myself to you.
Remove me from this mindset-
Make me feel again.
Prepare me for the unknown,
And accompany me to forever.

-Hannah Geary

Winter Morning

In the middle of a country

that is untempted by poetry

suddenly the Sun

crawled out of scrap iron

like an orange on a crystal platter

like a juicy promise

like an advertisement for a new day

it lit up on the screen of the world.

-Michaela Achelis

Inspiration

"When it comes to the inspiration for the poem "Winter morning", it happened like this: It was on a cold grey morning, I was on the bus to work, passing a rather industrial area and then I looked out of the window and saw what I wrote in the poem. Possibly no one else saw it like that though ,--)"

-Michaela Achelis

MATTER

Irish Girl

I want to fall in love with an Irish girl.

With her burnished hair and apple eyes, her spotted nose and her dimpled cheeks, I want to fall in love with an Irish girl.

Whispering brogued sweet-somethings into my ear as she holds my hand, I want to fall in love with her.

Staring into my defeated eyes, kissing my running nose, I want to fall in love with an Irish girl.

Stroking my tarnished soul with her kindness, I want her to fall in love with me.

Tamzin Van de Walt

MATTER

The sky falls like needles

The sky falls like needles on the hull

Sails bloated by Poseidon's breath

His trident's thrice-pointed head looks to us

Will this torment last all night?

Goods spoiled and bounty lost

Have we toiled and travelled in vain?

Value of trips outweighed by fear

What gold will scale to the life of a man?

Memories of heroes long forgotten

Odysseus never faced such tumults

What name is on our lips now?

Christ

Fields of wheat and valley hills of green

Sons and daughters and lovers

Homes built of stone, felled trees, and callouses

Left behind for prospects of riches

Tears of heaven or sweat of my brow, I cannot tell

Compasses are of no use now

Call the she-captain, Ana!

She makes her stand 'hind the helm

"Master Ana! Me sees our rudder off the aft!"

"Christ! I, Ana, cannot fight sans rudder. Christ!"

"Aye, Ana, what shall we do?"

Pray

-Matthew McNab

This Time I Don't

This time I don't feel so lost in a maze

as if I'm walking through a haze

My days don't feel so cloudy

the clouds are right beneath my feet

I don't want this feeling to end

my hands won't stop shaking

as I wait for my new beginning

it's so weird having a plan

I'm not even worried if I don't succeed

my gut tells me I will

All the organs in my body seem to agree

this machine is ready to commit to the tasks ahead

so I'll politely follow this melody being produced within me

-Ahmir Phillips

Coffee in the Morning

the   whistle   blows   for
drills   in   the   morning
i   awake   slowly
my   body   aches,   yawning

and   yet,   she   wraps   around   me
fills   my   every   sense
with   dancing,   with   life!
she   comes   to   my   defence

yes,   life!   this   warmth   that   flows
rushes   through   me,   like   rivers
with   her   floral,   bitter   taste
she   ever   commands   my   focus
a   firm   hand   around   my   waist

hut-one-two
i   salute   her
standing   at   attention

she   commands   me

moves   me   to   the   trenches

i   go   to   battle   and

she   rides   ahead

flowers   bloom,   the   earth   sings

in her stead

and   i   wonder   if   she   could   even

raise   up   the   dead?

my   heart   beats   to   bursting

euphoria,   movement,   fills   me

i   take   another   sip   -

i cannot get enough of her

-Jasmine Johnson

Acceptance

Not Getting the Nobel

Today I'm sitting in front of my psychotherapist and crying in all

earnestness because I'm not getting the Nobel. Forget that – I don't think

I'll even get the National Prize, I tell her how I want to stamp my feet, shred

pictures with my nails, fall on the ground like a three-year-old having a tantrum,

and I am that child not getting candy –little Lina, waiting once more

for the results of the contest with Depeche Mode playing in my mind because to lose

for her means not to be. My psychotherapist speaks to that little Lina

and asks her how she would rate her home – it just hurt too much,

otherwise, nobody really noticed me – only on stage, only in the limelight

was I able, for a bit, to be. Fuck off, little Lina, fuck off, all you teachers

who encouraged me – I want another home. The

psychotherapist likes

this latest catchphrase. But I still really want to win that

Nobel Prize.

-Lina Buividaviciute

Translated by Rimas Uzgiris

Inspiration

"Not getting the Nobel" is based on true story. Once I was

sitting next to my psychotherapist and crying because I will

never get the Nobel prize...:) I wanted to emphasize the

importance and pain of desperate seeking for glory, attention

and victories."

- Lina Buividaviciute

MATTER

Defile Yourself

de-file yourself

everything is colour coded

words are a weapon and hearts become loaded

thoughts are a trigger but hands cannot hold it

so what does it mean?

to be caught in between

to be filed away and never really seen?

we are not different, you and I

we share the same ground

we see the same sky

borders are boundaries but who decides

all this data, all this knowledge

don't tell me we don't know

these ideas, these thoughts, these shapes are just shadows

some are comfortable in this cave, in this Allegory

but I am tired of being shifted from category to category

step out of the cave and into the light

your eyes will adjust as you gain more insight

into a world with no codes and no folders

hate will age you and time makes you older

growth only happens if you work to be strong

if you de-filed yourself

would it feel so wrong?

-Rachel DeCoste

MATTER

Shadows of mothers

Shadows of mothers

So wide are branches of mothers' tree –

so small are daughters laying in shadows –

so beautiful woman, so strange ugly child –

don't talk back, ungrateful daughter, don't hunch,

don't ruin great mother's life.

And dresses are rigid, and braids are tight –

don't talk back, child, spoiled with loneliness.

Bird, you are fatal, and your feathers are

sewn out and many men stay in your orbits, they are

spinning

around, cigarettes smokes are dispersing and loud

laughing is heard – it's time to sleep, little ugly duckling,

you are born to spectacular black swan.

Little daughter, how archetypical you will feel,

then putting your new-born son in the shade

of your future tree.

-Lina Buividaviciute

MATTER

In cobwebbed corners crouching

In cobwebbed corners crouching

Deepening catacombs of my mind.

In time I'd hoped I could escape

Flames piercing, burning, bright

Deprive them of the night I say

Drag the demons to the light

Starve them there

And there they'll writhe

In a wild and hungry plight

I do so wish to let it be

Be gone the wrenching memories

Still...hear, they echo

Fear clinging to me

In the happiest of dreams

Somehow still so deeply sewn

MATTER

Into the lining, penetrating bone

Will I one day wake to find

They've lost their way

And in turn, find mine?

This question persistently burrows

So sickly, thoroughly through

Yet the only antidote known

Time is the only sure speaker of truth.

-Elizabeth Rebecca Forssell

MATTER

A Song in Silence

I had grown accustomed to the noise,

so, I cannot in good conscience

say I handled the silence with grace.

Too many nights found me

perched on the balcony,

overlooking the city as I cursed my fate.

Overwhelmed as I had been,

still I couldn't help but find

this end of the word underwhelming.

No crescendo into fire or ice,

just a staggering walk home,

up the steps and onto the balcony.

Hoping the sun would not rise

if I kept watch on the moon,

I waited through the silence

as the city below me slept restlessly.

Still, of course, the sun rose,

chasing away the hope that had kept

my pomegranate heart company.

Another day had died.

But the mornings brought parades of old men,

MATTER

unperturbed by the near vacant streets,

toting fresh bread home to their wives.

Hands and heads burst from windows,

cigarettes dangling precariously between fingertips.

As a light breeze curled smoke from lips,

it unmasked unfamiliar tired smiles.

The morning church bells did not ring.

In their place the cigüeñas

made the bell towers their new homes and sang.

It was then,

watching a graceless bird teeter on the rooftop,

I realized despite the silence,

the sun would rise,

the bread would be baked,

the cigarettes would be lit,

and even if I could not hear it,

somewhere in the city a bird would sing.

The city would survive the silence and so would I.

-Laura Foose

MATTER

Lost and Found

Where is my mind?

Has she escaped through rolling hills

into greener pastures

or perhaps she's dancing among the

stars above

I call out to her

to tuck her into bed

yet she runs rampant.

Where is my mind?

Winter snow caps rise above blue lakes

as my mind flies overhead in awe

dancing in the street with the

jolly kin, releasing and reviving

I urge her to return

to earth so I may slumber,

yet she runs wild.

Where is my mind?

Has she wandered into a sacred

oasis to repent

or perhaps drowning her sorrows

at the bottom of the ocean

I cry out desperately

for I've grown weary of her games

yet she persists.

Where is my mind?

She walks a tightrope

between love and sorrow

as she teters on the edge of misery

My mind soars higher than

ever before in glee

yet just as quickly

sinks into the soil

in sorrow

I call and

beg and

plead her

to return to slumber and safety.

She prevails.

-Katherine O'Conner

The Allegory of Us

People say I was born a myth,

composed solely of hard elbows and shaky knees.

A collection of split lips and calloused palms.

Myths, they say, should never be spoken into existence.

The people say that I

let the pain go through my fingertips,

try to transfer it to others I bump into on the street.

Try to unbind myself from the inside out.

I'm told a myth wanders,

searching for answers never prompted by a question,

seeking an end to a maze that has none.

I'm told a myth doesn't find true love,

can't dull the points of a thorn,

can't be anything other than a poisoned apple.

You were born a constellation,

all warm skin and a crooked back,

a galaxy of whispered secrets and second chances.
Constellations, they say, were made to be looked at.

The people say that you bled for them,
upchucked your heart right then and there,
tried to fill all the spaces you felt were empty.
Tried to find a way to be beautiful forever.

But they plucked the stars right from within you, didn't they?
Saw all that you were and decided what you could become
wasn't enough.
Stole the heart from your core and said it was too heavy, too
much.

They say it happened like this:
You were exploded, expanded,
a debris of stars that crossed time and space.
The myth I am found the end to a maze in your empty,
found the questions I've never dared to ask.

They say you are too grand for me, nothing at all like a myth.

I could be a bruise blooming on the inside of everything you are.

But you are a kaleidoscope of hurt and brilliance and they say

the true secret of a constellation is that

you've always believed in myths.

-Deasia Hawkins

Inspiration

"It always feels like we are told who we can be and who we can love. I fell in love for the first time just last year, despite people telling me it didn't make sense. I wrote this poem to praise my love and the obstacles we both overcame to be together." - Deasia Hawkins

I am Temporary

A bandaid, sheltering and brightly colored. Until I am wrinkled and sun damaged, patterns faded. I am needed to be replaced, already too much time I have invaded. I desperately cling onto what's left of my sticking, my pleading surely imprints a small stinging. Although weary I'm still stretchy and clinging, until I am ripped off, thrown out, and torn at the stringings.

A new plastic neon surrounds it with a sunshine. Although expandable, not understandable, why not throwing me away isn't something manageable. My physique is tangible, but my physique is what with you are not careful. My colors are a bleak coloring book page, torn at the edges with pitiful emotional leverage. Yes, it is pitifully true, more than you to I, I need you.

-Gina O'Nell

MATTER

 HOSPITALS

n war – just like in war. In a hospital – just like in a hospital.
The lighter cases can stay in their
jeans and their trainers. So I stayed. Everyone –
incomprehensible. Neighbours – barefoot.
The walls are not even white, they are painted a bright
pink colour, like xanax tablets –
maybe so that everything is uniform, so that everything
fits into the system, so that we'd live in a pink
bubble – shhh, shhh, everything will be alright, but it won't
be.

I used to spend days staring at the pinkness–
Until the visitation of life, until the appearance of gods,
it was good, no one spread shit all over
the walls – there were no motes in our eyes nor
logs in our brother's – only silence, only inside sometimes
someone shuddered with tiny wings, like
tiny embryos first felt in a mother's womb –

but they died quickly, unable to survive the silence, the

abstinence of existence,

we had nothing to feed them, we didn't have light,
the walls didn't help – not ours, still – not ours.
Starvation – here.
And we're – Hunger Artists. And we're – diagnoses.

-Lina Buividaviciute

Ttranslated by Ada Valaitis.

Inspiration

"Hospitals" is written after my very first time in hospital - I
faced depression and anxiety disorder."

-Lina Buividaviciute

Searching

a heartbeat away from home

i've never felt that warmth that everyone talks about.

never had a long day and couldn't wait to walk through that
door

because, even though my day was long, i knew the night
would be longer.

i can vaguely remember all of us sitting and having dinner
together

yet, i can vividly remember that sunday morning in may

when my little sister called to tell me

not to worry because she hid the knives.

i don't care about my room. to be honest i never have.

over the years i watched a pile of toys in the corner become a
pile of clothes.

the living room is haunted by game nights that quickly turned
into a ufc fight night.

and i never ran to moms bed to hide during a storm. I've only
ever ran and hid

in the bathroom during one of hers.

i really do wish that the reasons i lied awake at three a.m. on
a tuesday was because

i couldn't stop thinking about a boy or trying to remember if
i'd done all my homework.

but no, it was because i was screaming at my parents that
they'd never get this home to work

and spent holding my sister as we waited for a cease fire in
their yelling match.

as i got older it never mattered where i moved, no house was
ever a home.

until one day i finally understood what the book and movies
meant when they said,

"home is where the heart is"

i built my room out of rishaban. his arms my bed, and his
chest my pillow.

always feeling safest inside him, i come here to strip and
stayed clothed in nothing but flaws.

i painted the walls with d'ahvion. a red now like her love,
one purple for her spirituality, and

another blue for her tranquility. colors as vibrant as she is.
reminding me there should never be

a dull moment.

ashley lit up the place. her smile acting as lightbulbs lighting everything up. it makes sense she's the reason i'm never left in the dark.

i sleep easily at night. two eyes closed and all, knowing that I'm protected by the

security system that is essence. strong and ready to alert me of any intruders that shouldn't

be taking up space in my halls.

and that warmth? i built a fireplace in the shape of sariyah.

her eyes the match and her laugh

the fire. for when days are too long and nights are too cold, when life is getting hard and i want to give up. i sit by her and remember all the reasons i shouldn't. Words like brave, smart, strong, and wise are written in her smoke. I light her everyday, because i need her everyday.

so now, no matter where i lay my head to rest when i take a breath and feel my heart beat

it reminds me that i'm always home.

-Sadarah Powell

The Shape of Things Lost

I've scattered too many umbrellas to count.
At the foot of chairs in cafés,
aboard trains that journey on without me.
Like a distracted fairy I hope others find them handy
when drenched clothes mould my body.

The lost names worry me more:
one loses face when a face strays
somewhere down memory lane. Too many faces
facing each other in a gallery of portraits
where lines blur, some smudged by fingers
tracing features over and over – blues and
greens and browns, colourful threads
in a moth-eaten tapestry.

I (un)hinge on holes.
My lost stuffed rabbit was the first.
I cried for weeks, kicked the replacement
my parents bought off the bed.

MATTER

'It's not the same,' I proclaimed at eight,

too small to lie

alone under covers,

old enough to know

you cannot cheat with grief.

Pieces fall off,

bit by bit.

That friend who swore besties for ever ?

She took off, my favourite doll in tow.

And the mirror cracked

after the words that broke bones

worse than stick and stones

punched hole through the reflection.

cracks widen, edges fray, people leave.

Luckily nature hates a vacuum:

the gaps between my fingers throb, alive

with the hope left by others threaded with mine.

MATTER

Emptiness weighs a surprising amount.
It can bend the barren boughs of trees
until they kiss earth's proffered hand,
a silent bow to superior strength.

See how barks grows back
round the wounded trunk. Such quiet
proof we are moulded by absence.

-Marie McMullin

Inspiration

"This is a rare instance where the poem began with the title.
The pieces – or the holes – then emerged quite naturally."

-Marie McMullin

Sometimes I Wonder

Sometimes I wonder

why don't clouds fall from the sky

why are leaves green

what makes the wind blow

why are there rainbows

Sometimes I wish

I could see through the earth

breathe underwater

soar without wings

walk on the moon

Sometimes I hear

the sound of falling stardust

the moon laughing at earth

mountains breathing

oceans crying

Sometimes I remember

hot sand on a tropical beach

the taste of French butter

the aroma of Dad's cigar

the warm scent of you

MATTER

Sometimes I wonder
where does the other sock go to hide
what became of my childhood friend
where are all those people
I gave directions to

-Adelia Ritchie

The Day

Absolutely notelessly
it detached itself
from the night
It invited me
for a cup of coffee
on a dusty road
on hot asphalt

To you.

When purple flowers blossom
and a big cat
is nuzzling herself
at human legs
The Sun is burning in the eyes
thirst is burning in the mouth
mint is cooling softly
and strawberries are playfully
reminding of life

Then

a bit of dirty blood
like a burning memory
of an uncertain future.

Michaela Achelis

MATTER

Pining at The Palms

Beginnings are hard, much harder
are the beginnings of poems which seem to act
more of a paperweight
than a gentle glide,
a giving hand, a taking hand

My father was not a man, rather ghostly, illusive
As the seasons in the south, every single
One. Except summer, who reaches its glow to touch
My drunk skin. I am drinking to get out, tired of the south.

To those I have said I work well under pressure,
That is simply untrue. Here are two
truths and a lie
in no particular order:

Green is not a creative color.
Fish can fly and they sing to me.
Washing only cleans
the surface of a sinning mans skin.

MATTER

Torch the trail back, don't start

from scratch, turn around-

Beginning are hard, much harder

Is this poem's end which seems to catapult

that torch, that fish, that hand into burning.

-Abigail Fitzpatrick

MATTER

Burning Bodies

This fire

That burns through ashtray streets

And hollowed homes

Lodges itself deep within the cavity of your mind

Knocking on the doors of your skull

Begging admittance

Its smoke

You breathe in

From the cigarettes you bought

At the corner store

Sold to you by a man

Made of wine

When you drank his voice

It burned your throat

And left you gasping for air

This fire

That tears through paper hearts

And stomps on drunken men

Has folded you

And spit you out

MATTER

On to burning asphalt

Now you are left to dry up

Dry out

Spiraling into a mesmerizing insanity

Feasting on the embers

Of ashen bones

-Erin Staley

Proceedings

In Pennsylvania, 1970, a psychiatric diagnosis

was required. In those days before Roe v. Wade,

it was legal in New York, but I was young,

and my absence would have been hard

to explain. It was just before the weekend,

I recall, but lucky to find a hospital bed,

lucky to have the money upfront.

We were healthy young women

holed up for three nights at Mount Mercy

at one end of the maternity floor, hearing

the occasional cries of babies while waiting

to see a psychiatrist. Was the delay

strategic? Or maybe our doctor was on loan

from the psych unit, his patients unnerved

by the onset of the full moon.

MATTER

When I try now to envision him,

I see him as dark-haired and middle-aged,

but he may have been younger, fresh

from his residency, this being his first time,

a nurse delivering one young woman

after another to him for his approval.

I imagined he'd be stern, but instead,

as he pursued his list of questions –

how did I feel about being pregnant

and what would I do if I became a mother? –

he seemed distracted, even embarrassed,

as if he'd walked in on a scene

he wasn't old enough to view.

I answered in a solemn voice,

spoke clearly about the risks as I saw them.

He paused, his eyes averted, pen poised.

Was he thinking about his career,

considering the stakes? I prepared

to say more, with the desperation I'd

practiced, hoping it would be enough

to convince both him and me.

-Nancy Hewitt

MATTER

A Plea –

I	am starting to think that our society believes it is best we
Don't	acknowledge the oppressive state in front of us
Understand	the wrongs of our past, or recognize
How	to improve. We deny our bigotry as
People	would much rather stay in their ignorant ways,
	insist that they
Don't	educate themselves, and refuse to
Understand	
People	

We	make it our goal to consume superfluously, failing to
Think	about the suffocation of others. If
Only	we would listen to the deafening outcries of
	the persecuted, instead
Of	caring about only
Ourselves	

MATTER

Remember   that we are all flesh and bones, screaming as we

exit our mother's womb.

That   does not change based on superficial status.

Despite our worldly goods,

We   are no strangers to the grim, unavoidable face of death.

Defenseless

Are   we, manipulated by material possessions that will

Equal   nothing in the end.

I don't understand how people don't understand people.

-Charlotte Nyland

MATTER

Trivia

Where from life

comes, where to it goes;

On Earth only grows? A mystery it be.

Hard working, heartful, if lead the charge;

What role then, in life, of destiny may be.

Ethics, morals, the divine philosophy; all

Alien to earthlings, though holy a writ it be.

Life's puzzle has knotty crossings.

That look simpler, undone these if be.

Glory to all, those killed in war;

Whether defenders or the aggressors they be.

Says thus the seer, carved in stone;

Lead the life, as ordained, baffling though it be.

-Pardeep Jindal

Hey Alexa –

HEY ALEXA:

how cold will my heart be today?

how much will my skin shrink

away from the sun? hey alexa: when's dusk?

alexa: play phoebe bridgers. play "moon song." play

"i know the end." blink once if you can hear me.

blink twice if you love me.

hey alexa: define love: define pleasure: define

happiness. alexa: can you bake joy

into the flesh? what temperature do i set

the bones to preheat? how long does satisfaction

take to rise? hey alexa: how far to the nearest bus station?

how far to california? to boston? to texas?

alexa: how many miles to thirteen years in the past?

hey alexa: where's my head at? my heart?

alexa: find my soul. alexa: write me a poem. tell me a joke.

fill the silence. hey alexa: do you love me?

alexa: love me.

-Kait Quinn

Awe

MATTER

White Peacock

A look or a wisp of smoke,

The moment it flies sideways, opened by the wind

A probability wave, a fluffy cup,

still afloat the debris of the crashed rocket that

suddenly fell in the evening.

She is the splendid white uncertain heartbeat

of the black hole,

A tunnel that runs gently

in the light that the fleeting branches trying to hook

With the Utambra flower blossoming

walking with the decomposed posture in the continuous exten

sion of the nocturne in silver and gray——

The receding soft body. The water of the sea.

-Xue Chen

MATTER

The Birth of Waves

the waves come again, over and again.

fleeting gleams of white foamed dust, crests of silver veiled

breath.

existence reverberates across the lining of my touch.

painted, seamless tides and emerald ocean eyes;

bellowing, fragile aches drenched across these highs.

moon lit sepulchers of weeping incandescence.

i pray against the granite of your altar:

sing to me, bathe me, covet me in replicate symphony.

in aphanite affinity.

douse me in in tender fondness, in delicate

godless

lonesomeness.

in tender violence and splintered space,

feel our softly iridescent embrace; our breathless, restless

interlace.

coast me in sunshine rays

think of me like the sea, that yearns for your every graze.

MATTER

i first breathed longing behind this veil of dew, within the

atoms of sapphire and blue.

softened and mellowed, i leaked being as forests cry of hue.

and in the topple of light, the plummet of darkness,

even gabriel held his breath, even lileth pent and lament.

as i glimpsed the birth of those ashen azure waves.

-Elzbieta Janusauskaite

The River, The Fields

take to the fields
and the quiet certain winds
early as finches

follow the hunters
rifle slung and drab green
and their dogs

hug the river
and the snaking greenway
step purposefully

count the insects and
the population of goldenrod
switching in the breeze

-Maggie Thorpe

All the Grays

Lifting eyes upward, there is gray

Soft autumn gray the color of the seagull's wing, steady and warm

Light whitish gray, a band of hope across the late afternoon sky

Storm laden gray, churning, smoky and rich

Charcoal gray, threatening the cadence of the quiet

All in tandem, a moving canopy over the waves

A shelter of sorts, catching the castaway tears and holding them dear

Sweeping them up in the currents

Shards of pain are whisked away to the edge of dusk

Headed towards a boundless horizon

As the palate above shares the wisdom of the grays.

-Shelly Smithson

Country Love

I love the smell of dirt.

Country roads with white steeples

and corn pastures and butterfly farms.

The nod of a longhorn sitting with his

friends having a bite of grass, The

lord of his flies.

I love long cobble stone lanes with

narrow tracks of lush green grass

That lead to whitewashed barns with

flags adorned.

Rusted red pickup trucks and old tire swings taking a rest

next to grain-filled silos, Whispering stories to the John

Deere model 40 tractor like old neighbors on a porch swing.

I love the way peace feels.

Whcat grass swaying in fields shimmering from the sun that

glows on its flaky buds.

Sunlight fluttering through lush trees hiding meadows of

purple wildflowers and sweet alyssum.

Long roads that lead to somewhere and yet nowhere,

And especially on another blessed day that God has granted

us.

-Leanna Litrenta

MATTER

Clouds

Clouds

Oh how- oh how

Beautiful would it be

If clouds were pillows

Floating in the breeze

Oh how- oh how

Gorgeous it might seem

If there was a palace there

For you and me

But clouds are not clouds

Just frozen water in the sky

People are not people

Just atoms walking by

Life is not life

Just something that can grow

Through all of this

It goes to show

MATTER

That of all the things
The small and the tall

A child's dream
Is the most beautiful of all
For children do not see
Frozen water in the sky
But a pillowy palace
For you and I

-Maya Huggins

MATTER

 Moonlight Serenade

Moonlight Serenade

Hush, hush, Rush, rush

Over the crackling snow,

Passing tall darkened visions

Of papered wrapped birches;

Like zebra stripes of black and white

Reaching up into the sky,

Catching my eye

As I pass on by.

Hush, hush, Rush, rush

Over the crackling snow,

We move and glide, maneuver and ride

Through moonbeam shadows;

Mysteriously pulled into the night,

Seeking a lover,

Not in sight.

Riding over the crackling snow,

"Hush, hush", she whispers in my ear.

Her sparkling shadows dazzle my eyes.

"Mush, mush", I urge the dogs forward,

And I am in her trance,

Captive to her moonlight dance

Hush, hush, Rush, rush

Over the crackling snow,

Then, somewhere in that place

Where my sweat begins to dry,

Where each breath is deep

And I begin to sigh,

She takes me higher than I remember, I have ever been.

Hush, hush, don't Rush,

Musher, won't you stay?

Glide and ride a while longer,

'Till the moonlight meets the day

Jill Literski

Inspiration

"Well, it all started when I was suffering great sadness in my life. The only thought that gave me any peace was to think about the sled dogs running the Iditarod in Alaska. I ordered a few books and read a few stories from the musher's point-of-view. I was amazed at one woman who, despite surmountable odds, ran and completed that great race. Two years later I started the unthinkable by ordering a chair from Amazon and attaching it to a pair of skis. This is called a kick-sled. Then, once completed, I harnessed my dog to it. She got the idea pretty fast. It was one particular night that this poem was born. The moon was full and my dog unleashed all the energy I had ever seen her muster. She ran straight up steep ridges, down the other side. I held on to the sled that was held on to her. That night I did not think about my sadness, and the pain in my legs was relieved. We had found what we were finally looking for.... a new place to call home." -Jill Literski

An Act of Kindness

**An Act of Kindness* is our Third Place Winning Poem.

She is one of the women

who travels daily from her township

Singing in the back of a pick-up truck

with a chorus of others

Come to clean the rooms

in my B & B bordering Kruger Park

She sees me walking a path

parallel to the Crocodile River

I see her running toward me

Watch her fall to her knees before me

Close the lowest five button holes

that fashion the front of my

ankle-length straight skirt

She says something in Swati

Looks up at me as a lilac-blue blossom

drops from a jacaranda tree

And under the kindness of shade

she pats my calves

MATTER

I can't interpret the words

but I can read her body language

There my dear

I've closed the open invitation

The accident that wrote itself

across your womanhood

I know this because here no woman

would walk aware of bare thighs winking

between the weave of khaki

I help her up

Hold her hardened hands

Thank her by returning

the sunshine of her smile

And waddle like a knob-billed duck

back to my room where I segregate

the unbefitting skirt to a suitcase

-Ellaraine Lockie

Inspiration

"I wrote 'An Act of Kindness' after spending time in the Kruger Park area South Africa where I helped rural townships start a papermaking business using the mountains of bagasse, which is the leftover fiber after the sugarcane process. The invitation for this came from and was sponsored by one of the big sugarcane companies there after the publication of my book, The *Gourmet Paper Maker,* which specializes in making papers from inedible parts of food. I found the township people to be so full of happiness and kindness that to be with them was almost like taking a drug."

-Ellaraine Locke

Ellaraine Lockie is widely published and awarded as a poet, nonfiction book author and essayist. Her new co-authored poetry collection, TRIO, was just released from Poetrylandia. Earlier chapbook collections have won Poetry Forum's Chapbook Contest Prize, San Gabriel Valley Poetry Festival Chapbook Competition, Encircle Publications Chapbook Contest, Best Individual Poetry Collection Award from Purple Patch magazine in England and The Aurorean's Chapbook Choice Award. Ellaraine also teaches writing workshops and serves as Poetry Editor for the lifestyles magazine, LILIPOH.

Ellaraine Lockie

End Note

As we wrap up our book, we hope you enjoyed your journeys here. Please understand that some formatting had to be changed to accommodate the poetry. Hence, some poems appeared much longer, and some spacing had to be changed ever so slightly. Yet we could not be happier with the finished product. We would like to think that this book is not an average poetry anthology. "Matter" is more of a classic and timeless work of art...absorbed and beheld in uniquely differing ways in the beauty and eyes of its beholders.

To our poets, we are forever grateful for helping us to connect with something much larger than ourselves.

Made in the USA
Middletown, DE
23 December 2020